# The French and Indian War

Tammy Gagne

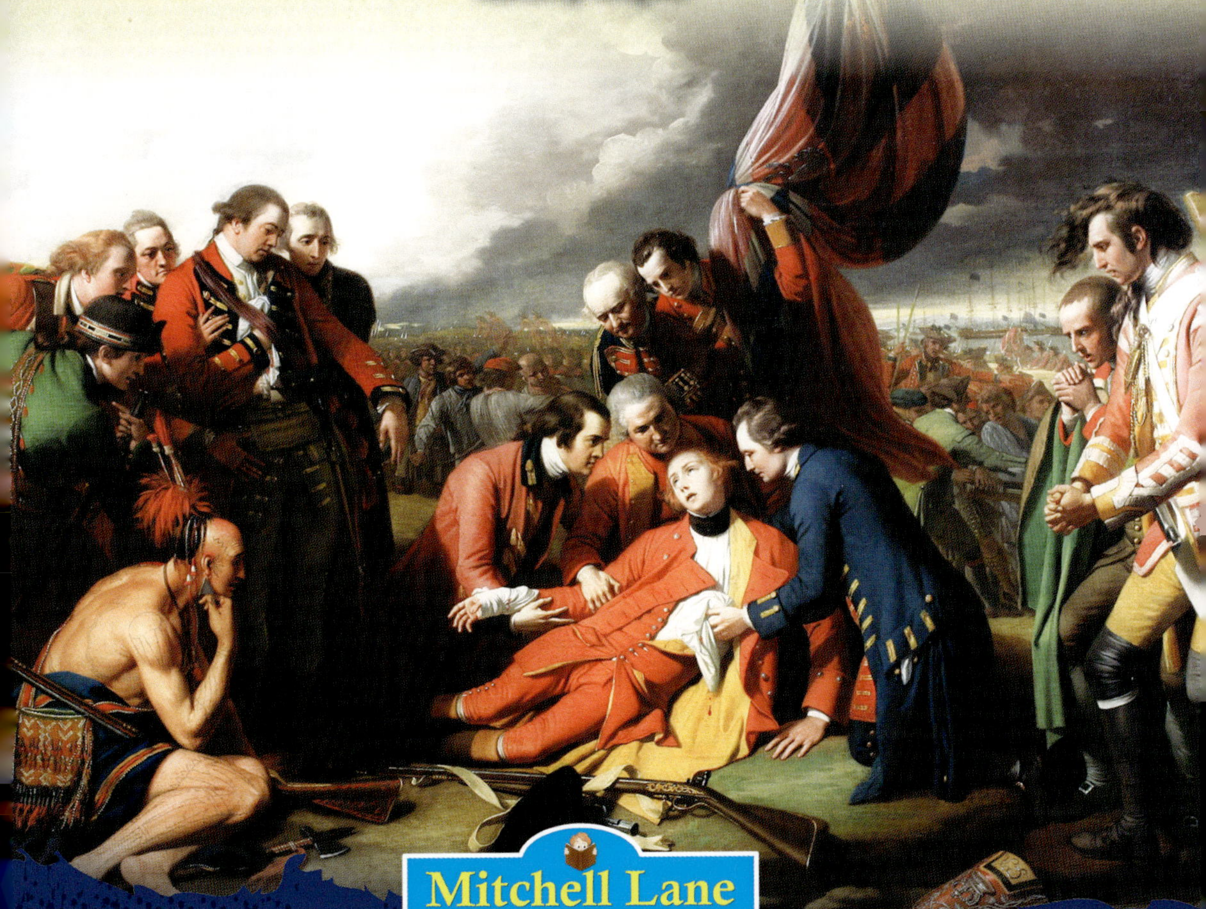

Mitchell Lane
PUBLISHERS
2001 SW 31st Avenue
Hallandale, FL 33009
www.mitchelllane.com

Printing 1 2 3 4 5 6 7 8

The First Continental Congress
**The French and Indian War**
Life in the Original 13 Colonies
The Second Continental Congress
Stamp Act Congress
The Story of the Declaration of Independence
An Overview of the American Revolution
Who Were the Signers of the Declaration of Independence?

**Library of Congress Cataloging-in-Publication Data**
Names: Gagne, Tammy, author.
Title: The French and Indian War / by Tammy Gagne.
Description: Hallandale, FL : Mitchell Lane Publishers, 2018. | Series: Young America | Includes bibliographical references and index. | Audience: Age 9-13. | Audience: Grade 7 to 8.
Identifiers: LCCN 2017009132 | ISBN 9781612289878 (library bound)
Subjects: LCSH: United States—History—French and Indian War, 1754-1763—Juvenile literature.
Classification: LCC E199 .G124 2017 | DDC 973.2/6—dc23
LC record available at https://lccn.loc.gov/2017009132

eBook ISBN: 978-1-61228-988-5

# CONTENTS



Words in **bold** throughout can be found in the Glossary.

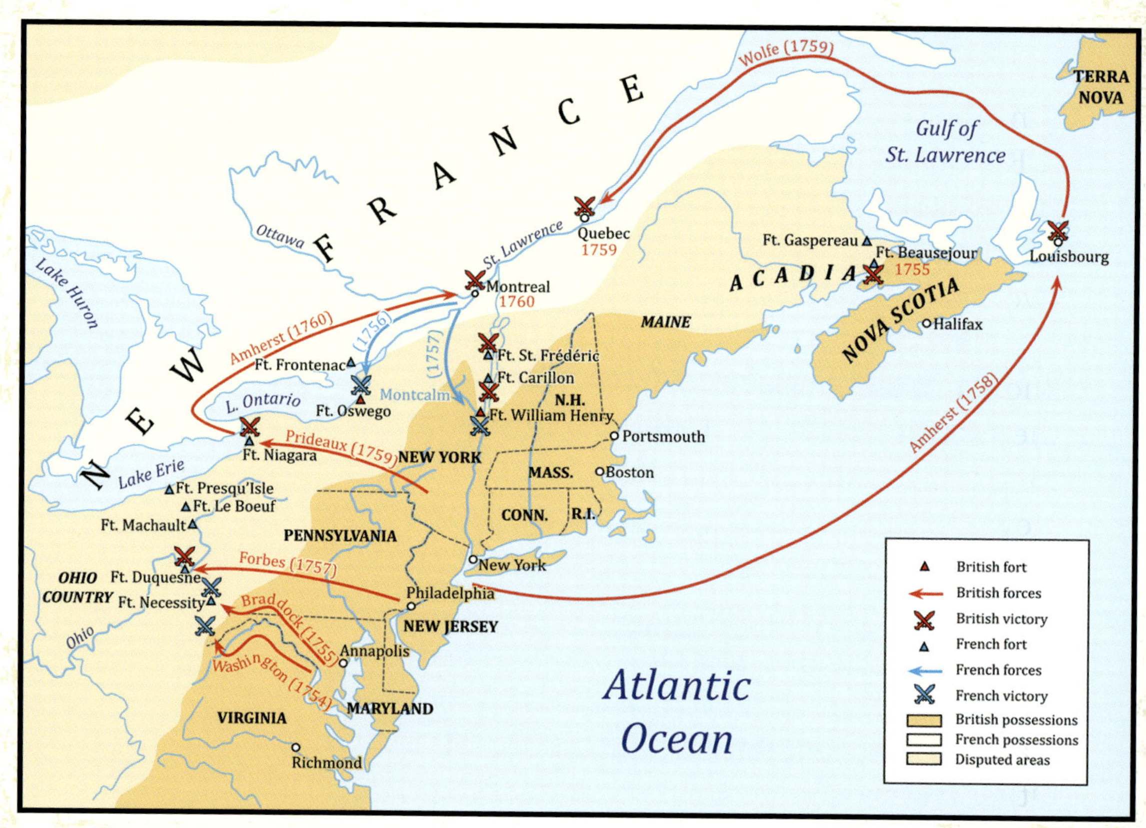


This map shows many of the important campaigns and major battles of the French and Indian War.

# 1

# Planting the Seeds of Conflict

In the early years of the seventeenth century, several European countries began crossing the Atlantic Ocean and establishing settlements in North America. By the turn of the century, France and England had emerged as the two leading powers on the continent.

New France, as the land claimed by the French was known, was a vast expanse of territory. It extended from the mouth of the St. Lawrence River on the Atlantic Ocean to the foothills of the Rockies, from the Great Lakes to New Orleans, where the Mississippi River empties into the Gulf of Mexico. Yet by the middle of the 18th century, only about 70,000 people occupied these millions of square miles. The largest settlements, Quebec City and Montreal, only had a few thousand people. Many of the rest were fur trappers and explorers who roamed the trackless forest. Others were soldiers who manned a series of forts.

The British, on the other hand, had established 13 colonies that occupied a relatively narrow strip of land between the Appalachian Mountains and the Atlantic seaboard. Their territory was only a fraction of the size of New France. Yet about a million and a half people lived there, and their numbers were steadily growing. Families had many children to help out on the farms, and increasing numbers of immigrants from other European countries were continuing to arrive. Cities such as Philadelphia, Boston, and New York had populations of at least 15,000 people.

France and Britain had been enemies for centuries. They had engaged in dozens of wars with each other, some major, some minor. The most recent conflict ended in 1748. But the subsequent peace was very fragile. It wouldn't take much to shatter it.

Nearly all the French forts were either along or near the St. Lawrence River in the east, and the upper Mississippi River and Great Lakes region to the west. In 1749, the British King George II granted a charter to the Ohio Company of Virginia. The charter allowed Virginia settlers to move westward into the Ohio Valley, in modern-day Ohio and western Pennsylvania.

This expansion alarmed the French. They regarded the Ohio Valley as part of New France. In early 1753, they began constructing several new forts, one on the south shore of Lake Erie and the others further south. These forts not only reinforced their claim to the territory but also served as a link to their older forts by preventing the colonists from driving a wedge between them.

In addition to these fortifications, the French had another advantage. They had powerful **allies** among many of the Indians living in the region. The Indians knew the land better than either the British or the French.

## George Washington Gets His Chance

Virginia's Governor Robert Dinwiddie was a major investor in the Ohio Company. In October 1753, he sent 21-year-old **militia** major George Washington and a few other men on

Virginia colonial governor Robert Dinwiddie

a mission from Virginia to the newly constructed Fort Le Boeuf. Washington's mission was to deliver a letter from Dinwiddie to the French commandant of the fort, Jacques Legardeur de Saint-Pierre. The letter began,

> The Lands upon the River Ohio, in the Western Parts of the Colony of Virginia, are so **notoriously** known to be the Property of the Crown of Great-

> Britain, that it is a Matter of equal Concern and Surprize to me, to hear that a Body of French Forces are erecting Fortresses, and making Settlements upon that River, within his Majesty's Dominions . . . it becomes my Duty to require your peaceable Departure.[1]

Washington had another task. Not all the Indians supported the French. He was to meet with a leader of the Iroquois, which was a confederacy of several important tribes that opposed the French, and seek his support in the likelihood of an open conflict. This leader was named Tanaghrisson, also known as the Half King.

Six weeks after setting out, Washington finally arrived at his destination and delivered Dinwiddie's letter to St. Pierre. The French leader scoffed at the message. He told Washington that the French had no intention of abandoning their forts or departing from the region.

The rejection of Dinwiddie's demands probably came as no surprise to Washington. Shortly before arriving at the fort, he had met a group of French officers. As he noted in his **journal**,

> They told me, That it was their absolute Design to take Possession of the Ohio, and by G[od] they would do it; for that they were sensible the English could raise two Men for their one; yet they knew, their Motions were too slow and dilatory to prevent any Undertaking of theirs. They pretend to have an undoubted Right to the River, from a Discovery made by one LaSalle 60 Years ago; and the Rise of this expedition is, to prevent our Settling on the River or Waters of it.[2]

Robert Chevalier de la Salle was a noted French explorer who had traveled extensively in North America during the seventeenth century. He claimed that territory for France.

Washington was alarmed at this report of increased French troop strength in the Ohio Valley. He returned to Virginia as fast as he could. He was fortunate to be alive. Harsh winter conditions had hindered his return. At one point he fell into a river choked with ice and had to scramble to safety. On another occasion, he was nearly shot by Indians who ambushed his party. They traveled nonstop through the night to get far ahead of their attackers.

**Fort Duquesne**

Dinwiddie believed that Saint-Pierre's rejection of his demand to leave the Ohio Valley was a hostile act. He immediately hatched a new plan. He sent several dozen men to build a fort where the Allegheny and Monongahela Rivers meet to form the Ohio River. It is where the city of Pittsburgh lies today. It was an important strategic location.

In that era, there were few roads in the wilderness. The rivers formed natural highways that facilitated the movement of people and goods. Controlling them was especially important. In mid-April, when the French realized what the British were doing, they attacked. The building party was greatly outnumbered and fled. The French made the captured structure much larger and stronger. They named it Fort Duquesne after the governor-general of New France, the Marquis Du Quesne.

In the meantime, Washington—now a lieutenant colonel—was en route to the fort with about 160 militiamen to reinforce it. When he was about 40 miles away, he learned that the French had taken it. He wasn't sure what his next step should be. That decision was soon made for him.

George Washington encounters Tanaghrisson, or the Half King, as he leads his troops toward Fort Duquesne in 1754.

# The Spark That Set Off the War

One of Washington's most important tasks was ensuring the continuing loyalty of his Iroquois allies. One method of achieving that goal was making sure they knew how badly the French wanted to get rid of Tanaghrisson. On May 27, 1754, Washington wrote in his journal, "I did not fail to let the young Indians who were in our Camp know, that the French wanted to kill the Half King; and that had its desired Effect."[1]

He knew that he had earned the Indians' loyalty—just as he had hoped. "They thereupon offered to accompany our People to go after the French," he continued, "and if they found it true that [Half King] had been killed, or even insulted by them, one of them would presently carry the News thereof to the [Iroquois], in order to incite their Warriors to fall upon them."[2]

That night, Washington received an urgent message from Tanaghrisson. The Half King said that a group of French soldiers was camped nearby. He urged Washington to link up with his warriors so they could launch a joint attack. As Washington wrote later,

> That very Moment I sent out Forty Men, and ordered my Ammunition to be put in a Place of Safety, under a strong Guard to defend it, fearing it to be a **Stratagem** of the French to attack our Camp; and with the rest of my Men, set out in a heavy Rain, and in a Night as dark as Pitch, along a Path scarce broad enough for one Man; we were sometimes fifteen or twenty Minutes out of the Path, before we could come to it again, and so dark, that we would often strike one against another: All Night long we continued our Rout.[3]

The combined force of militiamen and Iroquois Indians padded silently toward their unsuspecting quarry the following morning and took up their positions. Washington would launch the attack on one side of the French camp, with the Indians lying in wait on the opposite side.

### A Tough Call

One of the French soldiers spotted Washington's men and fired at them. Both sides began shooting at each other. A man standing next to Washington was killed. The Virginians quickly gained the upper hand and the French tried to retreat. But the Iroquois emerged from their place of concealment. Realizing they were surrounded, the French threw down their weapons and surrendered. The fighting had lasted barely 15 minutes. Its impact would reverberate for years.

The French leader—Joseph Coulon de Villiers du Jumonville—had been killed. It was widely believed that Tanaghrisson had buried a tomahawk in the man's head after he surrendered. The other French prisoners insisted that Jumonville had been a **diplomat**. They maintained that

he was on his way to warn British forces that they were encroaching into French territory and telling them to withdraw. This was almost exactly the same type of mission that Washington had undertaken just a few months earlier. This information made Washington's victory more complex. Diplomats were not supposed to be harmed. Diplomatic law provides them with protection. But Washington was unconvinced he had done anything wrong. He saw Jumonville as a spy.

Still, he was in a tough spot. "They say they called to us as soon as they had discovered us; which is an absolute Falshood," Washington wrote, "for I was then marching at the Head of the Company going towards them, and can positively affirm, that, when they first saw us, they ran to their Arms, without calling; as I must have heard them, had they so done."[4]

He also noted that letting Jumonville and his men go might have cost him the support of the Iroquois. "It was the Opinion of the Half-King in this Case, that their [French] Intentions were evil, and that it was a pure Pretence; that they never intended to come to us but as Enemies; and if we had been such Fools as to let them go, they would never help us any more to take other Frenchmen."[5]

## Washington Surrenders

Washington's victory at what became known as the Battle of Jumonville Glen was short-lived. Realizing that the French were likely to launch a counterattack, he established a post called Fort Necessity near the scene of the battle. Several weeks later, a large body of French troops from Fort Duquesne and hundreds of their Indian allies assaulted Washington's fort and inflicted severe casualties on his men.

Washington built Fort Necessity to defend his troops against French retaliation following the Battle of Jumonville Glen. But he chose a poor location, and a much larger French and Indian force forced him to surrender.

The French leader, who was Jumonville's brother, demanded Washington's immediate surrender. Otherwise, he added, the Indians might overwhelm the fort and scalp everyone inside. Washington agreed. He was fortunate that the French allowed him and his surviving troops to return home rather than imprisoning or even executing them in retaliation for Jumonville's death. Washington signed a surrender document, then he and his remaining men departed from the scene of the fighting on July 4. This date would assume a special significance exactly 22 years later, when the Declaration of Independence was ratified by the Second Continental Congress. By then Washington would be the commander-in-chief of the Continental Army.

The Battle of Jumonville Glen had a much more immediate impact. British historian Horace Walpole later wrote, "The volley fired by a young Virginian in the backwoods of America set the world on fire."[6] That's because the conflict between the two sides in the Ohio Valley helped launch a far more wide-ranging conflict known as the Seven Years War two years later. The Seven Years War pitted Britain and its allies against the French and their allies. While the main battlefields were in Europe, other fighting extended as far as India.

By then, the French and Indian War was well underway in North America. When the British government learned of the Battle of Jumonville Glen and Washington's subsequent surrender, they decided to send a military expedition led by General Edward Braddock to the colonies early the following year. Its objective would be to drive the French out of the Ohio Valley.

The French learned of this expedition and dispatched troops of their own to North America. They also used the surrender document Washington had signed at Fort Necessity to justify this action. It had been written in French, which Washington didn't know, and referred to the murder of Jumonville and his status as a diplomat. Therefore he hadn't realized that by putting it his signature on the document, he had confessed to committing an act of war. The fragile peace was about to end.

The British government sent General Edward Braddock to serve as commander of British forces in North America. He personally led an expedition against Fort Duquesne. He set out from Virginia in the spring of 1755. His troops included colonists, Indians, and George Washington.

# 3

# Dark Days and Years

The colonies were woefully unprepared for the coming conflict. Though they spoke a common language and shared many of the same customs and beliefs, the colonies regarded themselves as separate entities. With remarkable foresight, Benjamin Franklin—who would become one of the most important of the Founding Fathers—had tried to rally the colonists with a drawing and article in the *Pennsylvania Gazette*, the newspaper in Philadelphia he owned. It appeared less than three weeks before the Battle of Jumonville Glen.

The drawing depicted a snake sliced into eight segments. The snake's head had the initials N.E. (for New England) and the other seven were each labeled with the initials of a colony. The caption read "JOIN or DIE."[1] Franklin's goal was to show the colonists that if they remained separate, they were sure to lose the war that he and many other people believed was about to break out. But if they joined together, they would have a much stronger chance of conquering the French and their Indian allies. Franklin may have chosen the image of a snake because of the common superstition that a snake cut into pieces would

P.
N. E.
S. C.
M.
V.
N. Y.
N. J.
N. C.

JOIN, or DIE.

Benjamin Franklin's now-famous snake cartoon first appeared in the *Pennsylvania Gazette* on May 9, 1754. He labeled the head of the snake "N.E." for New England. Its other body segments symbolized seven of the other colonies.

reassemble itself if the pieces were laid together before sunset.

The *Pennsylvania Gazette* was perhaps the most prominent newspaper in the colonies. Because of its importance, other newspapers throughout the colonies printed Franklin's message in one way or another. The *Boston Gazette* used its own snake drawing with the words "Unite and Conquer" coming from the serpent's mouth.[2] Other newspapers described both the image and the saying.

Benjamin Franklin is considered one of the most influential Founding Fathers of the United States. This statue of him stands in Manhattan across from the New York Times Building. He holds a copy of his newspaper, the *Pennsylvania Gazette*.

## A Call for Unity

Franklin didn't stop there. He had been encouraged by the support and publicity the drawing had generated. So he and Massachusetts governor Thomas Hutchinson convened a congress in the New York town of Albany that June. It was perhaps the first effort to unite the colonies and seven of them sent delegates. "They [the delegates] then proceeded to sketch out a *plan of union*, which they did in a plain and concise manner, just sufficient to shew [show] their sentiments of the kind of union that would best suit the circumstances of the colonies, be most agreeable to the people, and most effectually promote his Majesty's service and the general interest of the British empire,"[3] Franklin explained.

He was disappointed when none of the colonial governments adopted the program that the congress drew up, known as the Albany Plan of Union. They thought it would lessen their power and authority and might even deprive them of some of their territory.

## Disaster in the Forest

The war got off to a disastrous start for the British. General Braddock, who had never led men in combat, was contemptuous about the fighting ability of his opponents. He decided to begin his campaign by attacking Fort Duquesne in June, 1755. As he neared his objective, he quickly found out how wrong his attitude was. Washington accompanied the expedition, and as he explained to Dinwiddie afterward,

> We were attacked (very unexpectedly) by about three hundred French and Indians. Our numbers consisted of about thirteen hundred well armed men, chiefly Regulars [British soldiers], who were

Braddock's troops were within seven miles of Fort Duquesne when they were ambushed. Many of them were killed or wounded in the confusion. Braddock was one of the dead men.

> immediately struck with such an inconceivable panic, but nothing byt [but] confusion and disobedience of orders prevailed among them. . . . And when we endeavoured to rally them, in hopes of regaining the ground and what we had left upon it, it was with as little success as if we had attempted to have stopped the wild bears of the mountains, or rivulets with our feet.[4]

Nearly a thousand soldiers were killed or wounded. Braddock was one of the dead. Washington narrowly missed being killed himself. Two horses he was riding were shot, and he had four bullet holes in his clothing. He helped lead the survivors to safety.

### Expressing the Fear of Indians

Braddock's defeat spread fear and distrust of the Indians among the colonists. In a sermon delivered a month later, Reverend Samuel Davies of Hanover, Virginia, addressed these issues:

> Our mother-country is at a great distance, and before we can receive help from thence, our country may be overrun, and fall a helpless prey to our enemies. We are **prodigiously** weakened, and our enemies strengthened, by the loss of our fine train of artillery; and the Indians will probably break off their alliance with the English and join the victorious party; and what **barbarities** we may expect from these treacherous and revengeful **savages**, I cannot think of without horror.[5]

Not all Indians were frightening to the colonists. The *Pennsylvania Gazette* published a statement by King Heigler, chief of the Catawba tribe. "The white People [British] and my People are like two Brothers that came out of one Womb, and we will live as such for ever," he said. "When I was at New York, to make Peace with the Six Nations [the Iroquois], I said, that I and my People would always fight against the Enemies of the white People."[6]

Not all the news was bad. In August, Indian agent William Johnson took a force of colonial troops into French territory. He changed the name of Lac du Saint-Sacrement to Lake George to honor the British monarch, then won a victory there. Afterward he built Fort William Henry at the south end of the lake to strengthen British defenses in the area.

Fighting was often brutal and barbaric. Colonist militiaman Robert Moses described the fate of two men who had had the misfortune to be captured by the Indians: "We received intelligence that a number of Indians supposed to consist of one hundred killed two men about two miles from the Fort, took the man's heart and cut it in two and laid it on his neck, and butchered the other most barbarously, sought a house near the Fort, wounded one man that he died about an hour after our arrival."[7]

**Montcalm's victories**

French and Indian forces commanded by General Louis-Joseph de Montcalm captured Fort Oswego, which lay near the southeastern corner of Lake Ontario, in August, 1756. He took 1,700 prisoners and burned the fort. With things continuing to go against the colonists, newspapers took on the task of convincing them that the French posed a major threat. Typical was an editorial in the *Virginia Gazette* that year. It declared,

The Battle of Fort Oswego was one of several early French victories in the French and Indian War. The fort was located on the Oswego River near Lake Ontario. The French have just hoisted their flag as a symbol of their triumph.

> Friends! Countrymen! . . . Awake! Arise! . . . When our Country, and all that is included in that important Word, is in most threatening Danger; when our Enemies are busy and unwearied in planning and executing their Schemes of **Encroachments** and Barbarity . . . when in short our All is at Stake . . . the Patriot Passions must be roused in every Breast capable of such generous Sensations. . . . Countrymen! Fellow-Subjects! Fellow-Protestants! To engage your attention, I need only repeat, Your Country is in Danger.[8]

The French successes continued in 1757, highlighted by the capture of Fort William Henry in August. Montcalm led a force of more than 7,000 men against just 2,200 defenders. Many of the attackers were Indians, to whom

Montcalm had offered large amounts of plunder. He surrounded the fort and slowly moved inward. The British had no hope of reinforcement and had to surrender.

Under those terms, the British garrison was allowed free passage away from the fort. The Indians attacked the retreating column and took their possessions, slaughtered some of defenseless men, women, and children, and kidnapped many more. The incident formed a major part of James Fenimore Cooper's 1826 novel *The Last of the Mohicans* and several movies based on the book.

While it wasn't apparent at the time, the capture of Fort William Henry marked the high-water mark of French victories. For one thing, the Indians were so unhappy with Montcalm's leadership that many of them decided not to help the French any longer. On the other hand, the colonists were so infuriated that they wanted to do everything possible to defeat the French. The course of the war was about to change.

**French general Louis-Joseph de Montcalm tries to stop his Indian allies from massacring British prisoners after the Battle of Fort Oswego.**

Montcalm and his men celebrate their victory at the Battle of Fort Carillon in the summer of 1758. It was the last major French victory in the war.

# 4

# Gaining the Upper Hand

Montcalm oversaw one final French victory. In early July the following year, British general James Abercrombie led a massive force of 16,000 troops against Fort Carillon, between Lake George and Lake Champlain. It was the largest number of troops under a single command in North America. Montcalm had less than 4,000 men. Yet Abercrombie committed so many **tactical** errors that historians would later use terms such as "incompetent" and "imbecile" to describe him. The British suffered well over 2,000 casualties to less than 400 for the French and were driven off. Soon afterward the French abandoned the fort. The English took control and renamed it Fort Ticonderoga.

Earlier that year, the British government had decided to send over several new commanders and thousands of additional troops. The colonies did their part as well. Assemblies in the northern states offered substantial enlistment bonuses that attracted volunteers in droves. For the first time since the war began, the colonists' regiments were at full strength. According to some estimates, the number of armed men on the British side—soldiers, sailors, and marines—was about the same as the total population of New France. The

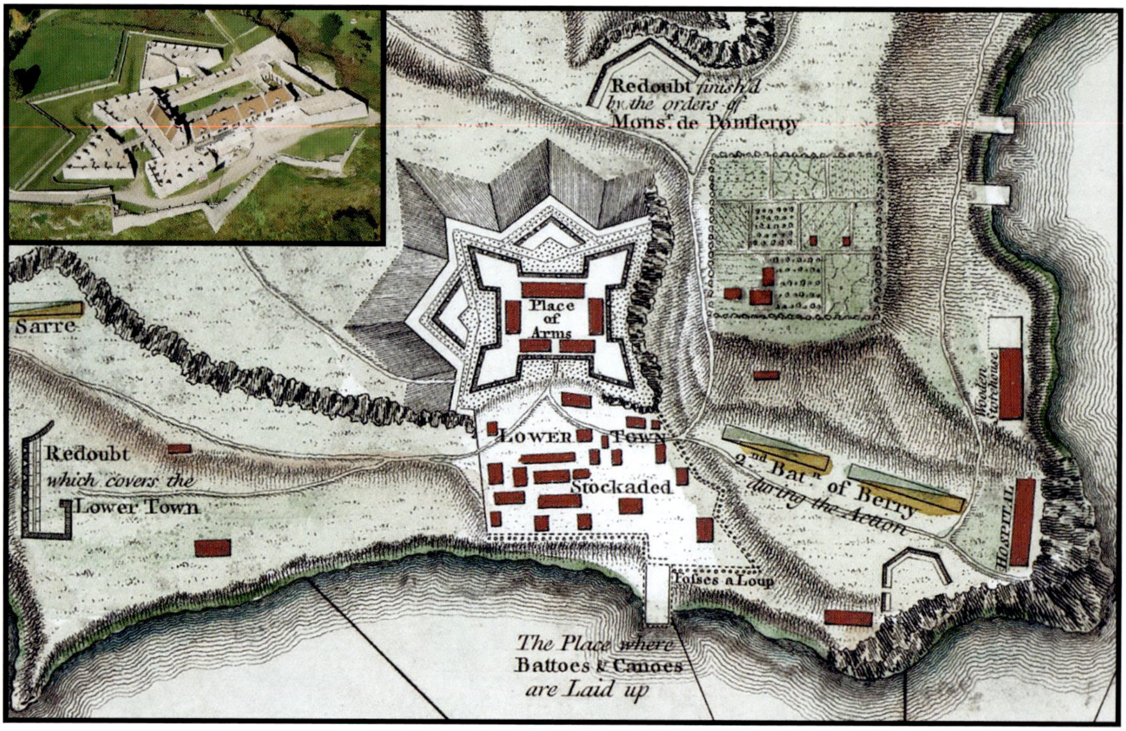

This image shows the plan of Fort Carillon. The British captured it in 1759 and renamed it Fort Ticonderoga. The inset shows the restored fort, which is open to visitors.

French, on the other hand, were afraid that any troops who tried to cross the Atlantic would be captured by Royal Navy warships, which had taken control of the high seas. They also needed them to fight closer to home in the Seven Years War.

Despite the disaster at Fort Carillon, the British soon gained the upper hand in the conflict. They began taking French forts.

## Taking Louisbourg

The first to fall was Louisbourg. It lay at the entrance to the St. Lawrence River and prevented British ships from entering the waterway. General Jeffery Amherst commanded

more than 25,000 men and nearly 200 ships. After a siege of about six weeks, the French surrendered in late July.

The British also gained control of the Ohio Valley. When they attacked Fort Frontenac—located near the eastern shore of Lake Ontario—in August 1758, only about 100 French soldiers remained to defend it. They were no match for the 2,500 troops the British had sent to do the job. The loss of the fort threw a wrench in the French lines of communication. As a member of the victorious British force pointed out,

> By the demolition of Fort Frontenac, the enemy have been depriv'd of their grand magazine, from whence their western territories, garrisons, and Indian allies were supplied with ammunition, provisions, and goods of all kinds. By the destruction of their fleet, the intercourse between Canada and Niagara, has in a great measure been cut off, and the dominion of the lakes wrested from their hands; by which, according to their own confession, they will be obliged to abandon their own settlements, forts, and possessions on lake Erie, the freights of lake Huron, and the lake Superiour; their trade and interest with the Indians inhabiting those countries, must consequently decay, and if a proper use is made of these advantages, may be utterly taken from them.[1]

The war was coming full circle. Shortly after the British took Fort Frontenac, an even larger force headed toward Fort Duquesne. One of the members of the force was George Washington. He had been busy during the time leading up to this expedition. Dinwiddie had promoted him

to colonel in 1755 and put him in command of a **regiment** of about 1,000 Virginians. Washington had wanted to attack Fort Duquesne but the size of his regiment was barely adequate to defend the colony's borders.

## Washington on the March

So now he was pleased to be a part of such a large body of troops as they covered the same ground that had nearly cost him his life just a couple of years earlier. At this point many of the French Indian allies had deserted them. But the French still had fight left in them. The *Pennsylvania Gazette* published a letter describing an attack in October on a British forward outpost at Loyal Hanning:

> The Engagement began at Eleven o'clock, A.M. and lasted till Two. They renewed the Attack **thrice**, but our Troops stood their Ground, and behaved with the greatest Bravery and Firmness at their different Posts, repulsing the Enemy each Time; **notwithstanding** which, they did not quit the Investment that Night, but continued firing random Shots during that Time. This has put our Troops in good Spirits.[2]

The "good Spirits" became even better late the following month when the remaining French soldiers realized they could not protect Fort Duquesne any longer. They abandoned the fort and burned it down. The fort that Washington had lost before his men could even claim it years earlier didn't lie in ruins for very long. The British erected a new fort on the site, naming it Fort Pitt after British political leader William Pitt the Elder. The modern city of Pittsburgh is named after him.

George Washington joins in the salute as the British flag is raised at Fort Duquesne in November, 1758.

The victory ended the threat to Virginia's borders. It also ended Washington's participation in the French and Indian War. He resigned his commission and went home. Nearly 17 years later he would resume his military career under very different circumstances.

Many high-ranking military officers were killed during the French and Indian War. One of them was General James Wolfe. Wolfe died during the Battle of Quebec in September, 1759. But he died knowing that his troops had won the battle.

# 5

# The End—and the Beginning

With the recent string of victories providing momentum, the British decided it was time to strike at the heart of French Canada, the region of Quebec. In turn, the heart of this region was its capital, Quebec City. It lay atop a 200-foot-high bluff overlooking along the St. Lawrence River. Just getting to the top of the bluff would be challenging. In addition, Montcalm had created a formidable defensive system.

Commanded by General James Wolfe, the British began moving toward Quebec in June, 1759. An early attack failed and the two sides settled down to face each other. With little else to do, some of Wolfe's troops began attacking lightly defended small settlements along the river. A sergeant-major—whose name is unknown—kept a diary that illustrated the "total war" nature of these attacks. On July 16, he wrote, "We set the Town on Fire, about 12 O'clock, which continued burning all that Day."[1] A similar entry came less than a week later. And nearly a month after that, he wrote, "On the 20th the Louisbourg Grenadiers began their March down the main Land of Quebeck, in order to burn and destroy all the Houses on that Side."[2]

Wolfe succeeded in gaining the heights on September 13. His men spread out along the Plains of Abraham, a flat area in front of the city. Montcalm came out to meet him. Wolfe was badly wounded during the fighting. Before he died, he learned that the French were retreating. "Now, God be praised, I will die in peace," he reportedly said. Montcalm was also wounded and died the next day. The French surrendered on September 18.

The following year the British took Montreal. It was the last significant engagement of the French and Indian War. The Seven Years War continued until early 1763, when the Treaty of Paris ended both conflicts. Great Britain assumed control of much of New France. The French retained only two small islands off the Canadian mainland.

## Second Chances

The end of the war created a second chance for the colonists and the Indians to improve their relations. Two years before the Treaty of Paris, a Chippewa chief named Minavavana spoke to British trader Alexander Henry about the shared future of their people in the New World. "Englishman, although you have conquered the French, you have not yet conquered us! We are not your slaves,"[3] the chief said. Minavavana thought that the British needed to make offerings to show their good intentions for the future. "Englishman, your king has never sent us any presents . . . wherefore he and we are still at war; and until he does these things we must consider that we have no other father, nor friend among the white men than the King of France."[4]

Despite his negative words, Minavavana concluded by making an offer of peace to Henry. "As a token of our friendship," he announced, "we present you with this pipe to smoke."[5]

Opportunities such as these were largely ignored. The Indians realized that many colonists—especially the constant stream of new arrivals—sought the opportunities that would be provided by moving west into their lands, which made them very uneasy. In addition, the Indians regarded the British as less trustworthy than the French. While the French generally respected the Indians—many French men married Indian women and lived among the various tribes into which they had married—the British often looked down on the Indians and treated them with contempt.

## Pontiac's Rebellion

An Ottawa Indian chief named Pontiac took advantage of this dissatisfaction during a council of war in April 1763. He forged an alliance among a number of tribes and began attacking British forts and isolated settlements in what became known as Pontiac's Rebellion.

Early in the conflict, a large group of Indians began a siege of Fort Pitt. Two chiefs negotiated with the defenders. When the chiefs prepared to return to the hundreds of warriors surrounding the fort, a local trader named William Trent noted that the defenders had a parting "gift" for them. "Out of our regard for them," he stated sarcastically, "we gave them two Blankets and an Handkerchief out of the Small Pox Hospital. I hope it will have the desired effect."[6] Trent may have gotten his wish. A smallpox **epidemic** spread through the Ohio Valley soon afterwards, killing a large number of Indians.

Pontiac's Rebellion lasted for more than a year. During that time the Indians killed about 2,000 civilians and 400 soldiers.[7] Indian casualties were not recorded.

Even before Pontiac's Rebellion had ended, many colonists turned their attention to a new enemy rising out of

Chief Pontiac joined his tribe with many others to attack British forts following the end of the French and Indian War.

the ashes—their own mother country. The financial cost for the British during the French and Indian War and the Seven Years War was extremely high. Once the wars were finally behind them, the British were left with enormous debts.

There was an additional expense. Pontiac's Rebellion provided clear proof that the British had to continue to station troops along the frontier to protect the colonists from Indian attacks.

## Steps Toward Revolution

The first step in this process involved the Molasses Act. It had been in effect since 1733 and imposed taxes on molasses imported from non-British foreign colonies, such as those in the Caribbean. British officials hadn't made much effort to enforce the act. When it expired at the end of 1763, the need for additional revenue resulted in passage of the Sugar Act early in 1764. The intent of the Sugar Act was to "put teeth" into the Molasses Act by increasing enforcement of the tax and making it harder to avoid payment.

There were two problems. First, it soon became obvious that the Sugar Act wasn't going to raise much money. Second, the colonists objected violently to being taxed without having any say. The situation became worse the following year when the British government approved the Stamp Act.

Anger over the increasing taxes, increasing tensions between the colonists and the British troops, and the colonists' desire for more control over their own affairs would all play important roles in the following decade as the colonies moved toward independence.

There was another carryover from the conflict with the French. The British had emerged as the most powerful European power. The French were humiliated by their defeat. They looked for ways to exact revenge and regain some of their power and prestige. The Revolutionary War would eventually provide them with an opportunity to achieve those goals. The colonists, who had detested and feared the French just a few years earlier, would seek assistance from their former enemies in their bitter struggle against their former protectors.

The French and Indian War was over. But the battles for the British colonists had just begun. They would culminate in 1783 with the creation of the new United States of America.

# APPENDIX

## FRENCH AND INDIAN WAR TIMELINE

**1744–1748**

King George's War

This event, which precedes the French and Indian War, occurs between Great Britain and France. Both nations strive for control of North America. Neither country emerges a clear victor. King George's War ends with The Treaty of Aix-la-Chapelle.

**1752–1753**

Rising tensions between Great Britain and France

The two sides compete for land in North America, with small fights in many rural areas.

**November–December 1753**

George Washington's warning

Washington delivers a warning to Captain Jacques de Saint-Pierre at Fort Le Boeuf to stop encroaching on land claimed by Great Britain in Virginia. The French captain ignores the demand.

**May 28, 1754**

The Battle of Jumonville Glen

Washington, his soldiers, and their Indian allies carry out a surprise attack on the French. Following their success, Washington constructs Fort Necessity.

**July 3, 1754**

The capture of Fort Necessity

About 600 French soldiers, aided by about 100 Indians, attack Fort Necessity. Washington is outnumbered and surrenders.

# APPENDIX

## FRENCH AND INDIAN WAR TIMELINE

**July 17, 1754**
Washington's resignation
Accepting the blame for losing Fort Necessity, Washington resigns his commission.

**July, 1755**
Virginia Regiment is formed
George Washington is named as colonel of the regiment.

**July 9, 1755**
Battle of the Wilderness
French and Indians defeat General Edward Braddock near Fort Duquesne and kill hundreds of his soldiers.

**September 9, 1755**
The Battle of Lake George
Colonel William Johnson becomes the first British hero of the French and Indian War when his forces defeat the French at the Battle of Lake George.

**May, 1756**
A mutual declaration of war
British and French declare war, beginning the Seven Years War.

**August, 1756**
Capture of Fort Oswego
Combined French and Indian forces capture this fort on the shore of Lake Ontario and take 1,700 prisoners.

# APPENDIX

## FRENCH AND INDIAN WAR TIMELINE

**August 8, 1757**

Fort William Henry falls

Louis-Joseph de Montcalm, the commander-in-chief of the French army in North America, captures Fort William Henry. Some British soldiers and civilians are massacred after the battle.

**July 8, 1758**

Fort Carillon attack

French defenders of Fort Carillon in New York repel a major British attack.

**July 26, 1758**

The taking of Louisbourg

The British take Louisbourg, which opens up the St. Lawrence River as a way of attacking Quebec and Montreal.

**August 27, 1758**

Surrender at Fort Frontenac

French soldiers surrender to the British at Fort Frontenac on Lake Ontario. The move cuts off French communications with their fellow troops in the Ohio Valley.

**October 21, 1758**

Peace between the British and the Indians

The British make peace with the Delaware, Iroquois, and Shawnee Indians.

**November 26, 1758**

The retaking of Fort Duquesne

The British recapture Fort Duquesne, renaming it Fort Pitt.

# APPENDIX

## FRENCH AND INDIAN WAR TIMELINE

**June 26, 1759**
Fort Carillon falls
British troops drive out a handful of French defenders and capture the fort.

**July 25, 1759**
The western frontier
With the taking of Fort Niagara and Crown Point, the British control the western frontier.

**September 13, 1759**
Battle of Quebec
The British defeat the French in a battle that takes the lives of both commanders, French General Montcalm and British General Wolfe.

**September 8, 1760**
Montreal surrenders
Faced with overwhelming numbers of British troops, the French surrender the city

**September 15, 1760**
The British win control of Montreal. This final victory leads to the French surrender of Canada.

**1761**
The British make peace with the Cherokee Indians.

**February 10, 1763**
The Treaty of Paris
The British receive all French land east of the Mississippi River, with the exception of New Orleans. The Spanish receive all French land west of the river.

# CHAPTER NOTES


**Chapter 1: Planting the Seeds of Conflict**

1. Letter from Virginia's Governor Dinwiddie to the French Commander in the Ohio Country, October, 1753. ExplorePAhistory.com. http://explorepahistory.com/odocument.php?docId=1-4-1A

2. George Washington, *Major GEORGE WASHINGTON's Journal to the River OHIO, etc.* (October 31, 1753). http://www.earlyamerica.com/earlyamerica/milestones/journal/journaltext.html

**Chapter 2: The Spark That Set Off the War**

1. George Washington, *Expedition to the Ohio, 1754: Narrative.* Founders Online. http://founders.archives.gov/documents/Washington/01-01-02-0004-0002

2. Ibid.

3. Ibid.

4. Ibid.

5. Ibid.

6. Jack Kelly, *Band of Giants: The Amateur Soldiers Who Won American Independence* (New York: Palgrave Macmillan, 2014), p. 5.

**Chapter 3: Dark Days and Years**

1. David A. Copeland, "Fighting for a Continent: Newspaper Coverage of the English and French War for Control of North America, 1754-1760." http://www.earlyamerica.com/review/spring97/newspapers.html#notes

2. Ibid.

3. "Benjamin Franklin, Reasons and Motives for the Albany Plan of Union." The Founders' Constitution. http://press-pubs.uchicago.edu/founders/documents/v1ch7s2.html

4. George Washington: The Soldier Through the French and Indian War. Historic Valley Forge. http://www.ushistory.org/valleyforge/washington/george1.html

5. Samuel Davies, "In Times of War" (sermon), July 20, 1755. http://www.sermonindex.net/modules/articles/index.php?view=article&aid=27341

6. *The Pennsylvania Gazette*, June 16, 1757. http://www.ncpublications.com/colonial/newspapers/subjects/FIW.htm#1757

7. Robert Moses, *Diary of Robert Moses Kept During the French and Indian War.* The Gilder Lehrman Institute of American History. http://www.gilderlehrman.org/collections/cb0a2cd4-e876-4c93-92d2-366324483270

8. David Sloan and Lisa Mullikin Parcell, *American Journalism: History, Principles, Practices* (Jefferson, NC: McFarland & Company, 2002), p. 229.

# CHAPTER NOTES

### Chapter 4: Retaking Fort Duquesne

1. *Account of Lieut. Col. Bradstreet's Expedition to Fort Frontenac, by a Volunteer on the Expedition*. Openlibrary.org. http://www.archive.org/stream/impartialaccount00brad#page/n7/mode/2up

2. *The Pennsylvania Gazette*, October 26, 1758. https://books.google.com/books?id=aQcMAAAAYAAJ&pg=PA392&lpg=PA392&dq=%27but+continued+firing+random+Shots+during+that+Time.+This+has+put+our+Troops+in+good+Spirits%22+pennsylvania+gazette&source=bl&ots=TjIleHGPYI&sig=KAGXOHBFqlcCD2xdd5A9awrvQ8c&hl=en&sa=X&ei=JwKrVIzWPMyzggTA30DIDA&ved=0CCEQ6AEwAA#v=onepage&q=%27but%20continued%20firing%20random%20Shots%20during%20that%20Time.%20This%20has%20put%20our%20Troops%20in%20good%20Spirits%22%20pennsylvania%20gazette&f=false

### Chapter 5: The End—and the Beginning

1. Henderson, Robert (editor). "A Soldier's Account of the Campaign on Quebec." The Seven Years War Website. http://www.militaryheritage.com/quebec1.htm

2. Ibid.

3. Minavavana, a Chippewa chief, addressing trader Alexander Henry, as recorded by Henry, 1761. http://www.smithsoniansource.org/display/primarysource/viewdetails.aspx?TopicId=&PrimarySourceId=1183

4. Ibid.

5. Ibid.

6. Harold B. Gill, Jr. "Colonial Germ Warfare." Colonial Williamsburg. http://www.history.org/Foundation/journal/Spring04/warfare.cfm

7. Ibid.

## FURTHER READING

Collier, James and Christopher Collier. *The French and Indian War: 1660-1763.* Kindle Edition. Bath, UK: AudioGo, 2012.

Maestro, Betsy. *Struggle for a Continent: The French and Indian Wars 1689-1763.* New York: HarperCollins, 2000.

McClung, Robert. *Young George Washington and the French and Indian War, 1753-1758.* North Haven, CT: Linnet Books, 2002.

Santella, Andrew. *The French and Indian War.* New York: Children's Press, 2011.

Smolinski, Diane. *Battles of the French and Indian War.* Chicago: Heinemann, 2003.

## WORKS CONSULTED

*Account of Lieut. Col. Bradstreet's Expedition to Fort Frontenac, by a Volunteer on the Expedition.* Openlibrary.org. http://www.archive.org/stream/impartialaccount00brad#page/n7/mode/2up

Anderson, Fred. *The War that Made America: A Short History of the French and Indian War.* New York: Penguin Books, 2005.

"Benjamin Franklin, Reasons and Motives for the Albany Plan of Union." The Founders' Constitution. http://press-pubs.uchicago.edu/founders/documents/v1ch7s2.html

Cave. Alfred A. *The French and Indian War.* Westport, CT: Greenwood, 2004.

Copeland, David A. "Fighting for a Continent: Newspaper Coverage of the English and French War for Control of North America, 1754-1760." Archiving Early America. http://www.earlyamerica.com/review/spring97/newspapers.html#notes

Davies, Samuel. "In Times of War" (sermon), July 20, 1755. http://www.sermonindex.net/modules/articles/index.php?view=article&aid=27341

George Washington: The Soldier Through the French and Indian War. Historic Valley Forge. http://www.ushistory.org/valleyforge/washington/george1.html

Gill, Harold B. "Colonial Germ Warfare." Colonial Williamsburg. http://www.history.org/Foundation/journal/Spring04/warfare.cfm

Henderson, Robert (editor). "A Soldier's Account of the Campaign on Quebec." The Seven Years War Website. http://www.militaryheritage.com/quebec1.htm

Kelly, Jack. *Band of Giants: The Amateur Soldiers Who Won American Independence.* New York: Palgrave Macmillan, 2014.

# WORKS CONSULTED


Moses, Robert. *Diary of Robert Moses Kept During the French and Indian War*. The Gilder Lehrman Institute of American History. http://www.gilderlehrman.org/collections/cb0a2cd4-e876-4c93-92d2-366324483270

Minavavana, a Chippewa chief, addressing trader Alexander Henry, as recorded by Henry, 1761. Smithsonian Source. http://www.smithsoniansource.org/display/primarysource/viewdetails.aspx?TopicId=&PrimarySourceId=1183

*The Pennsylvania Gazette*, June 16, 1757. http://www.ncpublications.com/colonial/newspapers/subjects/FIW.htm#1757

*The Pennsylvania Gazette*, October 26, 1758. https://books.google.com/books?id=aQcMAAAAYAAJ&pg=PA392&lpg=PA392&dq=%27but+continued+firing+random+Shots+during+that+Time.+This+has+put+our+Troops+in+good+Spirits%22+pennsylvania+gazette&source=bl&ots=TjIleHGPYI&sig=KAGXOHBFqlcCD2xdd5A9awrvQ8c&hl=en&sa=X&ei=JwKrVIzWPMyzggTA30DIDA&ved=0CCEQ6AEwAA#v=onepage&q=%27but%20continued%20firing%20random%20Shots%20during%20that%20Time.%20This%20has%20put%20our%20Troops%20in%20good%20Spirits%22%20pennsylvania%20gazette&f=false

Relive: French and Indian War History. http://www.warforempire.org/relive/the_history.aspx#how_begin

Seven Years' War, History.com. http://www.history.com/topics/seven-years-war

Sloan, David and Lisa Mullikin Parcell. *American Journalism: History, Principles, Practices*. Jefferson, NC: McFarland & Company, 2002.

Washington, George. *Expedition to the Ohio, 1754: Narrative*. Founders Online. http://founders.archives.gov/documents/Washington/01-01-02-0004-0002

Washington, George. *Major GEORGE WASHINGTON's Journal to the River OHIO, etc.* (October 31, 1753). http://www.earlyamerica.com/earlyamerica/milestones/journal/journaltext.html

"Young George Washington Sets out on a Diplomatic Mission—Through the Wilderness." The Schiller Institute, November, 2011. http://www.schillerinstitute.org/educ/hist/eiw_this_week/v3n46_nov13_1753.html


**PHOTO CREDITS**: All design elements from Thinkstock/Sharon Beck. Cover, p. 1—Benjamin West/Public domain; p. 4—Hoodinski/cc by-sa 3.0; p. 7—National Portrait Gallery/Public domain; pp. 10, 31—Classic Image/Alamy Stock Photo; pp. 14, 16, 21—North Wind Picture Archives/Alamy Stock Photo; pp. 18, 25—Library of Congress; p. 19—Beyond My Ken/GFDL/cc by-sa 4.0 International; pp. 24, 36—Public domain; p. 26—Henry Alexander Ogden/Public domain; p. 28—Thomas Jefferys/Public domain, (inset)—Charny/cc by-sa 3.0; p. 32—Benjamin West/William Wollett/Library of Congress.

# GLOSSARY

**barbarity** (bahr-BAIR-uh-tee)—cruelty

**diplomat** (DIP-luh-mat)—person employed or skilled in the work of keeping up relations between the governments of different countries

**encroach** (en-KROHCH)—to enter another's property or rights little by little

**epidemic** (ep-uh-DEM-ik)—an outbreak of disease that affects large numbers of people

**journal** (JUHR-nuhl)—personal record of events

**militia** (mi-LISH-uh)—a body of citizens with some military training who are called to active duty in an emergency

**notorious** (noh-TAWR-ee-uhss)—generally known and talked of

**notwithstanding** (not-with-STAN-ding)—despite

**prodigious** (pruh-DIJ-uhss)—very big

**regiment** (REJ-uh-muhnt)—a military unit usually consisting of several companies

**savage** (SAV-ij)—a person belonging to a group with a low level of civilization

**stratagem** (STRAT-uh-juhm)—a trick in war for deceiving and outwitting the enemy

**tactical** (TAK-tuh-kuhl)—relating to the arrangement and movement of forces in combat

**thrice** (THRISE)—three times

**undeniable** (uhn-di-NIE-uh-buhl)—plainly true

# INDEX

# About the Author

Tammy Gagne is the author of numerous books for adults and children, including *Who Were the Signers of the Declaration of Independence?* for Mitchell Lane Publishers. She resides in northern New England with her husband and son. One of her favorite pastimes is visiting schools to speak to kids about the writing process.